PREHISTORIC WORLD

TRIASSIC LIFE

Dougal Dixon

All inquiries should be addressed to:
Barron's Educational Series, Inc.
250 Wireless Blvd.
Hauppauge, New York 11788
www.barronseduc.com

Library of Congress Control Number: 2005938243

ISBN-13: 978-0-7641-3481-4
ISBN-10: 0-7641-3481-7

Printed in China
9 8 7 6 5 4 3 2 1

CONTENTS

INTRODUCTION

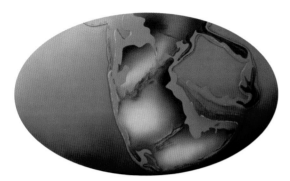

This map shows how the Earth looked in the Triassic Period. All of the continents were grouped into one mass of land.

This map shows how the Earth looks today. See how different it is! The continents have split up and moved around.

Prehistoric World is a series of six books about the evolution of animals.

The Earth's history is divided into sections called periods. These periods last millions of years. Each book in this series looks at the most important periods in prehistory.

This book looks at the Triassic Period, a time when reptiles were common in the seas, the sky, and on the land. This is when the first dinosaurs and the ancestors of the mammals started to evolve.

PREHISTORIC WORLD TIMELINE

Use this timeline to trace prehistoric life. It shows how simple creatures evolved into more different kinds. This took millions and millions of years. That is what MYA stands for – millions of years ago.

ERA	BOOK	PERIOD	
CENOZOIC ERA	THE ICE AGE	1.75 MYA to now QUATERNARY	This is a period of ice ages and mammals. Our direct relatives, Homo sapiens, also appear.
CENOZOIC ERA	ANCIENT MAMMALS	65 to 1.75 MYA TERTIARY	Giant mammals and huge, hunting birds appear in this period. Our first human relatives also start to evolve.
MESOZOIC ERA	CRETACEOUS LIFE	135 to 65 MYA CRETACEOUS	Huge dinosaurs evolve. They all die by the end of this period.
MESOZOIC ERA	JURASSIC LIFE	203 to 135 MYA JURASSIC	Large and small dinosaurs and flying creatures develop.
MESOZOIC ERA	TRIASSIC LIFE	250 to 203 MYA TRIASSIC	The "Age of Dinosaurs" begins. Mammals also start to appear.
PALEOZOIC ERA	EARLY LIFE	295 to 250 MYA PERMIAN	Sail-backed reptiles start to appear.
PALEOZOIC ERA		355 to 295 MYA CARBONIFEROUS	The first reptiles appear, and tropical forests develop.
PALEOZOIC ERA		410 to 355 MYA DEVONIAN	Bony fish evolve. Trees and insects appear.
PALEOZOIC ERA		435 to 410 MYA SILURIAN	Fish with jaws develop, and land creatures appear.
PALEOZOIC ERA		500 to 435 MYA ORDOVICIAN	Primitive fishes, trilobites, shellfish, and plants evolve.
PALEOZOIC ERA		540 to 500 MYA CAMBRIAN	First animals with skeletons appear.

5

 PSEPHODERMA

By the time of the Triassic Period, there were all kinds of animals living on land. There were also many that returned to the sea and found it easier to live there. The placodonts were a group of reptiles that lived in the sea and ate shellfish. *Psephoderma* had a long, pointed snout and strong jaws. It was ideally adapted for picking shellfish off reefs and crushing them with its broad teeth.

Psephoderma

Psephoderma had
a shell on its back
and looked rather like a turtle.
You can see the shell in this fossil.
However, *Psephoderma* was not closely related
to the turtles. It evolved a similar shape and
shell because it had a similar lifestyle.

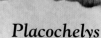

Placochelys

Henodus

NAME: *Psephoderma* (rough skin)

PRONOUNCED: sef-oh-der-ma

GROUP: Placodont – a group of swimming shellfish-eaters

WHERE IT LIVED: The seas around Southern Europe

WHEN IT LIVED: Late Triassic Period (223 to 209 million years ago)

LENGTH: 5 feet (1.5 meters)

SPECIAL FEATURES: Turtle-like shell on the back and another over the hips

FOOD: Shellfish

MAIN ENEMY: Other big swimming reptiles and shark-like fish

DID YOU KNOW?: Not all placodonts had shells. Some looked like giant newts. One relative, *Placodus*, was 6.5 feet (2 meters) long.

The placodonts in this picture all had armored backs. Their shells would have protected them from the other sea-living reptiles of the time – some of which were much larger and fiercer.

NOTHOSAURUS

Nothosaurus was one of the earliest sea-living reptilian hunters. Its feet were webbed, like those of a seal, and it had quite a long neck and long toothy jaws – just right for snatching at fish. It had a long tail to help it to swim. Even though *Nothosaurus* spent most of its time in the water, it had to come to the surface to breathe.

Ceresiosaurus

There were several types of nothosaur. *Lariosaurus* was one of the smallest, about 24 inches (60 cm) long. *Ceresiosaurus* and *Nothosaurus* were bigger and adapted better to life in the sea. They had long necks that made it easier to catch fish and feet that were used like paddles.

Lariosaurus

Nothosaurus

Fossils of nothosaurs – the group to which *Nothosaurus* belonged – have been found all over the world. *Nothosaurus* was the most common and widespread of them.

SHONISAURUS

Among the reptiles that returned to the sea, probably the most famous are the ichthyosaurs – the "fish-lizards." These were so well adapted to living in the sea that they could not have spent any time on land. Some of the earliest forms, like *Shonisaurus*, were truly enormous – truly whale-sized.

Shonisaurus was the biggest sea animal of the Triassic Period. One species, *Shonisaurus sikanniensis*, was 69 feet (21 meters) long. Its fossil was found in a remote river bank in Canada.

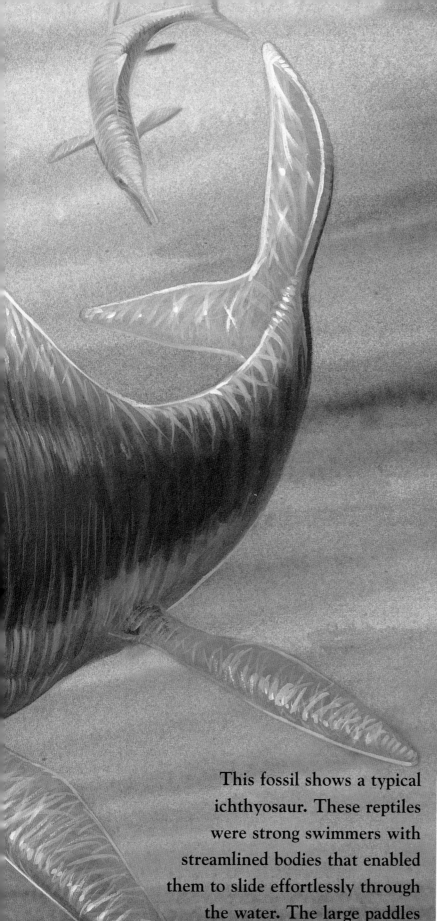

ANIMAL FACTFILE

NAME: *Shonisaurus* (lizard from the Shoshone Mountains, Nevada)

PRONOUNCED: shon-ee-sawr-us

GROUP: Ichthyosaur — the "fish-lizards"

WHERE IT LIVED: The sea that covered parts of the U.S. and Canada in Triassic times

WHEN IT LIVED: Late Triassic Period (235 to 223 million years ago)

LENGTH: 50 feet (15 meters)

SPECIAL FEATURES: Its size! It was the biggest ichthyosaur known

FOOD: Fish and sea-going invertebrates, like ammonites

MAIN ENEMY: None

DID YOU KNOW?: Scientists think that *Shonisaurus* only had teeth when it was young. Adults were toothless.

This fossil shows a typical ichthyosaur. These reptiles were strong swimmers with streamlined bodies that enabled them to slide effortlessly through the water. The large paddles were actually fingers that had become joined together.

EUDIMORPHODON

Toward the end of the Triassic Period, the reptiles mastered the skill of flying. Until then there had been a few lizard-like reptiles that were able to glide for long distances. But now the pterosaurs appeared – reptiles that could fly by flapping their wings like birds. *Eudimorphodon* was one of the first of the pterosaurs.

The pointed front teeth of *Eudimorphodon* were ideal for catching fish as it flew low over the surface of quiet lagoons. The smaller teeth at the back of the mouth would have gripped the slippery prey firmly while it was taken back to land to be eaten.

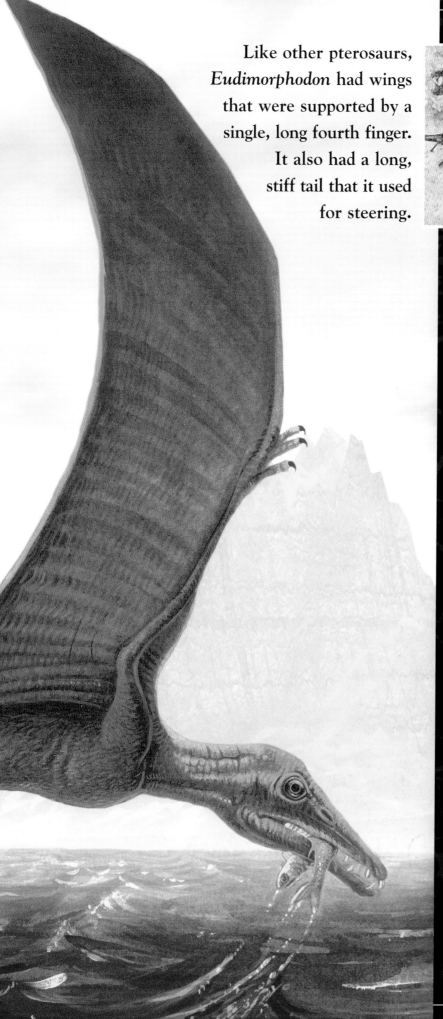

Like other pterosaurs, *Eudimorphodon* had wings that were supported by a single, long fourth finger. It also had a long, stiff tail that it used for steering.

ANIMAL
FACTFILE

NAME: *Eudimorphodon* (with two very differently shaped teeth)

PRONOUNCED: you-dee-morf-oh-don

GROUP: Pterosaur — the flying reptiles

WHERE IT LIVED: Italy

WHEN IT LIVED: Late Triassic Period (235 to 208 million years ago)

BODY LENGTH: 2 feet (0.6 meters)

WINGSPAN: 3.3 feet (1 meter)

SPECIAL FEATURES: Two different types of teeth

FOOD: Fish

MAIN ENEMY: Big fish and big reptiles

DID YOU KNOW?: One fossil of a close relative, *Preondactylus*, was found as a bundle of bones coughed up by a fish that had eaten it over 200 million years ago.

DESMATOSUCHUS

Before the dinosaurs evolved, the largest land animals were relatives of today's crocodiles. Some of these animals, like *Desmatosuchus*, were actually plant-eaters. They fed on ferns and other low-growing vegetation. These plants could be found near the oases of the desert landscapes of the time.

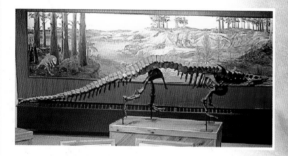

The back of *Desmatosuchus* was covered in rows of armor plates. Long spikes curved outwards from the shoulders and neck, helping to protect it against fierce predators, such as the meat-eating, land-living crocodiles.

ANIMAL FACTFILE

NAME: *Desmatosuchus* (link crocodile)

PRONOUNCED: des-mat-oh-sue-kus

GROUP: Aetosaur — a group of plant-eating crocodiles

WHERE IT LIVED: Arizona, Texas

WHEN IT LIVED: Late Triassic Period (233 to 223 million years ago)

LENGTH: 15.75 feet (4.8 meters)

SPECIAL FEATURES: Long spines on the shoulders for protection

FOOD: Low-growing plants

MAIN ENEMY: Carnivorous, land-living crocodiles

DID YOU KNOW?: *Desmatosuchus* was a very early member of the plant-eating crocodile group.

Desmatosuchus had weak, blunt teeth and a short snout like a pig. Its head was held close to the ground where the vegetation grew.

ARIZONASAURUS

The fiercest meat-eaters in Triassic times were big, land-living crocodiles like *Arizonasaurus*. They did not sprawl, like modern crocodiles, but walked on straight legs, like dogs. They prowled around the desert landscapes hunting the big plant-eating reptiles that lived in the oases of the time.

The sail may have kept *Arizonasaurus* warm, by taking in heat from the sun in the chilly mornings. This would have made it more active than its slow-moving prey, and would have helped it to hunt.

The first fossils of *Arizonasaurus* were found in 1947, but the scientists of the time thought they were just dinosaur bones. It was not until 2000 that it was realized the fossils came from a type of crocodile, not a dinosaur. The new animal was named *Arizonasaurus*.

ANIMAL
FACTFILE

NAME: *Arizonasaurus* (lizard from Arizona)

PRONOUNCED: a-riz-oh-na-sawr-us

GROUP: Rauisuchian — a group of land-living crocodiles

WHERE IT LIVED: Arizona

WHEN IT LIVED: Middle Triassic Period (240 to 230 million years ago)

LENGTH: 10 feet (3 meters)

SPECIAL FEATURES: Tall sail on its back

FOOD: Plant-eating reptiles

MAIN ENEMY: Bigger, land-living crocodiles

DID YOU KNOW?: *Arizonasaurus* looked rather like *Dimetrodon*, an earlier reptile with a sail on its back. In fact, these two reptiles are not closely related. They look the same because their lifestyles were similar.

ORAPTOR

In late Triassic times, many of the big land animals were crocodile relatives and other reptiles. The first dinosaurs were really quite small. *Eoraptor* was only the size of a fox, but it was an ancestor of the huge and magnificent dinosaurs to come.

This copy of an *Eoraptor* skull shows its long jaws and sharp teeth, just like those of later meat-eating dinosaurs. *Eoraptor* was also the same general shape as later predators. Its small body was carried on two strong hind legs. The arms were smaller with grasping fingers, and its neck was long and flexible. A long, heavy tail helped the dinosaur to balance.

ANIMAL
FACTFILE

NAME: *Eoraptor* (early hunter)

PRONOUNCED: ee-oh-rap-tor

GROUP: Theropod dinosaur

WHERE IT LIVED: Patagonia in South America

WHEN IT LIVED: Late Triassic Period (228 million years ago)

LENGTH: 3.3 feet (1 meter)

SPECIAL FEATURES: The earliest dinosaur known

FOOD: Small animals and insects

MAIN ENEMY: Big, land-living crocodiles

DID YOU KNOW?: Later meat-eating dinosaurs had three, or even two, fingers on the hand. Like its ancestors, *Eoraptor* still had five, although two of them were tiny. Changes like this help scientists to trace the evolution of dinosaurs.

Although *Eoraptor* was not very big, it was very active and fierce. It hunted small creatures of the time, such as reptiles and insects.

UNAYSAURUS

Dinosaurs quickly evolved into two groups: the meat-eaters and the plant-eaters. *Unaysaurus* was one of the earliest of the plant-eating groups. Like other dinosaurs of the time, *Unaysaurus* was smaller than many other animals around. Its later descendants were much bigger – they were the massive, long-necked sauropods such as *Brachiosaurus*.

Unaysaurus had teeth that were roughly serrated, like vegetable graters. It ate plants that grew on the ground and probably also stood on its hind legs, to reach leaves high up in trees.

Part of the *Unaysaurus* skeleton found in Brazil in 2004. From this, scientists can see that the hind legs of *Unaysaurus* were much longer and heavier than its front legs. This suggests that it was able to spend a lot of time on its hind legs.

ANIMAL
FACTFILE

NAME: *Unaysaurus* (Black Water lizard, named after the area where it was found)

PRONOUNCED: you-na-sawr-us

GROUP: Prosauropod dinosaur

WHERE IT LIVED: Brazil

WHEN IT LIVED: Late Triassic Period (225 to 200 million years ago)

LENGTH: 7.9 feet (2.4 meters)

SPECIAL FEATURES: The earliest known of the long-necked plant-eaters

FOOD: Leaves and ferns

MAIN ENEMY: Big, land-living crocodiles and early dinosaurs

DID YOU KNOW?: *Unaysaurus* was closely related to other dinosaurs found in North America, Germany and China. This shows the same kinds of animals lived all over the world at that time.

ANTETONITRUS

Antetonitrus was one of the first of the sauropods, a group of really big, long-necked plant-eaters. The sauropods evolved from the more primitive prosauropods in the late Triassic Period. *Antetonitrus* looked like the bigger members of the prosauropods. We can tell it was not the same by the different arrangement of bones in its feet.

Some of the trees of the late Triassic Period had tough sword-like leaves. This was to defend themselves against the new plant-eaters like *Antetonitrus*.

NAME: *Antetonitrus* (before the thunder – the later sauropods are sometimes called the "thunder lizards")

PRONOUNCED: ant-ee-tone-ite-rus

GROUP: Sauropod dinosaur

WHERE IT LIVED: South Africa

WHEN IT LIVED: Late Triassic Period (215 million years ago)

LENGTH: 26–32 feet (8–10 meters)

SPECIAL FEATURES: The earliest sauropod known

FOOD: Leaves and twigs from the trees

MAIN ENEMY: Meat-eating dinosaurs and land-living crocodiles

DID YOU KNOW?: When scientists first dug up *Antetonitrus* they thought that it was just another prosauropod. Twenty years later a new researcher looked at the bones and realized this was a completely new dinosaur.

Later dinosaurs like *Camarasaurus* (pictured) looked very similar to *Antetonitrus*. *Camarasaurus* had a claw on the inner front toe to defend against predators. Perhaps *Antetonitrus* also had this adaptation.

COELOPHYSIS

The early meat-eating dinosaurs may have been small, but some of them made up for this in cunning. *Coelophysis* was one of the earliest of the meat-eaters. There is evidence that it hunted in packs. Pack-hunting animals can successfully hunt beasts much larger than themselves.

Coelophysis was probably a scavenger as well as a hunter, and ate almost anything it could find. Many types of fish and reptiles have been found in its stomach.

Two forms of *Coelophysis* fossil have been found. One form is thinner and more delicate than the other. It is thought they are male and female dinosaurs.

ANIMAL
FACTFILE

NAME: *Coelophysis* (hollow form)

PRONOUNCED: see-low-fye-sis

GROUP: Theropod dinosaur

WHERE IT LIVED: Arizona and New Mexico

WHEN IT LIVED: Late Triassic Period (225 to 220 million years ago)

LENGTH: 10 feet (3 meters) — but most was neck and tail, and its body was about the same size as a fox

SPECIAL FEATURES: Lived and hunted in packs

FOOD: Other reptiles

MAIN ENEMY: Big, land-living crocodiles

DID YOU KNOW?: A fossil skull of *Coelophysis* was taken on the space shuttle *Endeavor* in 1998. It was the first dinosaur in space!

LILIENSTERNUS

By the end of the Triassic Period, some of the dinosaurs were quite large. *Liliensternus* was one of the first big hunters. It was big enough to hunt and eat the earliest of the long-necked plant-eaters.

In 1802, footprints were found in some Triassic rocks in Connecticut. They were thought to have been made by giant birds. However, after the discovery of fossils, such as this *Liliensternus*, it was realized that they were the footprints of meat-eating dinosaurs.

ANIMAL FACTFILE

NAME: *Liliensternus* (from Hugo Ruele von Lilienstern – an early palaeontologist who originally discovered the fossils)

PRONOUNCED: lil-ee-en-ster-nus

GROUP: Theropod dinosaur

WHERE IT LIVED: Germany, France

WHEN IT LIVED: Late Triassic Period (225 to 213 million years ago)

LENGTH: 20 feet (6 meters)

SPECIAL FEATURES: Large meat-eater with two crests on the head

FOOD: Other dinosaurs

MAIN ENEMY: None

DID YOU KNOW?: *Liliensternus* may have preyed on larger dinosaurs that were stuck in quicksand.

Two *Liliensternus* dinosaurs attack a prosauropod. This picture shows the crests on *Liliensternus's* head. It seems to have had two crests that ran from the nostrils to behind the eyes. They would have been used by the dinosaurs for signaling to each other.

CYNOGNATHUS

One group of reptiles became very similar to mammals in Triassic times. They were probably warm-blooded, like mammals, and had a similar body shape. They might have even had fur. Eventually this group evolved into the mammals themselves, in the Triassic Period. *Cynognathus* was one of the most mammal-like of these reptiles.

Scientists think *Cynognathus* was covered in fur because the bones of its snout show tiny pits where whiskers would have been. Only furry animals have whiskers.

The skull of the *Cynognathus* is very similar to the skull of a mammal. Only the shape of the jaw shows that it was actually a reptile.

ANIMAL
FACTFILE

NAME: *Cynognathus* (dog jaw)

PRONOUNCED: sy-nog-nay-thus

GROUP: Therapsid group of mammal-like reptiles

WHERE IT LIVED: South Africa

WHEN IT LIVED: Middle Triassic Period (245 to 230 million years ago)

LENGTH: 5 feet (1.5 meters)

SPECIAL FEATURES: Teeth like a dog, with nipping incisors at the front, stabbing canines at the side, and meat-shearing molars at the back

FOOD: Other animals

MAIN ENEMY: The big, land-living crocodiles

DID YOU KNOW?: The jawbone of *Cynognathus*, or something closely related, has been found in Antarctica. This shows that Africa and Antarctica were joined together in Triassic times.

Aetosaur — a group of plant-eating reptiles, very closely related to the crocodiles. They were covered in armor, and lived on land in the Triassic Period.

Ichthyosaur — the group of sea-going reptiles that were so well-adapted to living in the sea that they looked like dolphins or sharks, with fins on the tail and back and paddles for limbs. They were common in the Triassic and the Jurassic periods, but died out in the Cretaceous.

Nothosaur — a sea reptile that had long jaws for catching fish and webbed feet for swimming through water. Several kinds of nothosaur lived in the shallow waters around Europe and Asia in the Triassic Period.

Placodont — a group of swimming reptiles that fed on shellfish. Many had shells like turtles, although they were not related.

Prosauropod — an early dinosaur group that were plant-eaters and had long necks for reaching into trees. They were the biggest animals of the Triassic and early Jurassic, but not as big as their descendants — the sauropods.

Pterosaur — the flying reptiles of the age of dinosaurs. They had broad leathery wings, supported on a long fourth finger, and were covered in hair to keep them warm.

Rauisuchian — a group of land-living meat-eaters of the Triassic Period, closely related to the crocodiles. They were the fiercest animals of the time.

Sauropod — the plant-eating dinosaur group that had huge bodies, long necks, and long tails. They were the biggest land-living animals that ever lived, and reached their peak in late Jurassic times.

Therapsid — the most mammal-like group of the mammal-like reptiles. They were covered in fur, and had teeth like the teeth of a mammal. Some were so mammal-like that you would think they were dogs.

Theropod — the meat-eating dinosaur group. They all had the same shape — long jaws with sharp teeth, long strong hind legs, smaller front legs with clawed hands, and a small body balanced by a long tail.

LOSSARY

Adapted — changed to survive in a particular habitat or weather conditions.

Canines — strong, pointed teeth.

Carnivorous — an animal that eats meat.

Cunning — clever at getting what they want.

Dinosaur — large group of meat-eating or plant-eating reptiles that no longer exist.

Evolution — changes or developments that happen to all forms of life over millions of years as a result of changes in the environment.

Evolve — to change or develop.

Fossils — the remains of a prehistoric plant or animal that has been buried for a long time and has become hardened in rock.

Incisors — sharp-edged front teeth in the upper and lower jaws.

Lagoons — shallow ponds joined to seas or lakes.

Molars — special teeth used for grinding food.

Oases — green areas in a desert. They contain water and plant life.

Predators — animals that hunt and kill other animals for food.

Primitive — a very early stage in the development of a species.

Prosauropod — late Triassic Period ancestors of long-necked, plant-eating dinosaurs.

Reefs — ridges of rock, sand, or coral near the surface of the sea.

Reptiles — cold-blooded, crawling, or creeping animals with a backbone.

Reptilian — animals that look like a reptile.

Serrated — having a jagged edge like a saw.

Snout — an animal's nose.

Species — a group of animals which all look like each other.

Streamlined — an animal with a smooth, bullet-shaped body that allows it to move through air or water easily and quickly.

Trilobites — early type of sea animals, no longer existent.

Warm-blooded — animals, such as small mammals, which always have the same body temperature.

INDEX

PICTURE CREDITS

T = top, B = bottom, R = right, L = left

Main illustrations: 18-19 Lisa Alderson; 6-7, 8-9, 10-11 Simon Mendez;
22-23, 24-25, 26-27, 28-29 Luis Rey; 12-13, 14-15, 16-17, 20-21 Chris Tomlin

4TL, 4TR, 5 (Cenozoic Era), 6, 9, 11, 13, 14, 18, 21, 25, 26, 29 Ticktock Media archive; 5 (Mesozoic Era top,
Paleozoic Era top) Simon Mendez; 5 (Mesozoic Era center, Paleozoic Era bottom) Luis Rey; 5 (Mesozoic Era bottom)
Lisa Alderson; 17 Chris Tomlin; 23 Phil Degginger/Carnegie Museum/Alamy

Every effort has been made to trace the copyright holders and we apologize in advance for any unintentional omissions.
We would be pleased to insert the appropriate acknowledgment in any subsequent edition of this publication.